MATH GAMES
FOR THE COMMON CORE

Grade 2

Operations • Algebraic Thinking • Base Ten

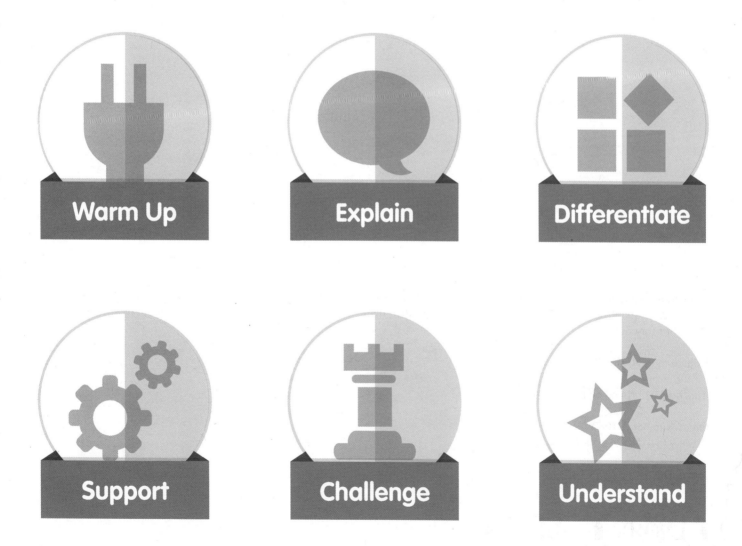

Warm Up

Explain

Differentiate

Support

Challenge

Understand

Gail Gerdemann with **Kathleen Barta**

Printed in the United States of America.

This book is printed on recycled paper.

Order Number 211080
ISBN 978-1-58324-659-7

A B C D E 18 17 16 15 14

395 Main Street
Rowley, MA 01969
www.didax.com

Table of Contents

Teacher Notes

Introduction

Math Games for the Common Core targets these domains of the Grade 2 Common Core State Standards:

- Operations and Algebraic Thinking
- Number and Operations in Base Ten

These games are designed to help students understand key concepts and strengthen skills. Developing number sense can take time. We all know that students are more engaged when they are having fun, and these games are designed for both substance and fun.

The *Math Games* program is also designed to be straightforward for teachers. Supplies include standard equipment like paper clips and colored markers, as well as copies of blackline masters. All materials for the year may be duplicated and organized in less than two hours. Basic manipulatives such as tiles and fraction pieces are recommended but not required.

The animated presentation files involve students in reviewing the key concepts and mathematical vocabulary they will need to play the games. They also teach the students how to play each game. The visual approach of the presentation files and the differentiated games make this program ideal for all students, including English Language Learners and Tier II students.

Each game unit provides:

- Ideas for more support and for more challenge
- Discussion questions to help students:
  - Make connections between the game and mathematical concepts
  - Engage in CCSS Mathematical Practices
- Straightforward directions
- Blackline masters

These games may also be used for home-school activities. The presentation files will make family math events easy to organize. During family math gatherings, be sure to share the ideas for more support and more challenge with parents. They will appreciate understanding how to adapt the games to meet their children's special needs.

Teacher Notes

Materials

It will take less than two hours with a high-speed copier and a paper cutter to prepare and organize a year's worth of materials for this program.

Step 1: Duplicate the blackline masters and place them in file folders.

Step 2: Duplicate cards on index-weight paper; cut the cards.

Step 3: Gather the recommended manipulatives.

Blackline masters (BLMs) begin on page 57. They are also on the CD.

Note on Number Cards: Regular playing cards may be substituted. Remove Kings, Jacks, and 10s. Use the Aces as 1 and the Queens as zero. ("Q" looks similar to "0.")

Bibliography

Carpenter, T., Fennema, E., Franke, M. L., Levi, L., & Empson, S. B. (1999). *Children's Mathematics: Cognitively Guided Instruction*. Portsmouth, NH: Heinemann.

Dougherty, B. J. (Ed.). (2010). *Developing Essential Understanding of Number and Numeration for Teaching Mathematics in Prekindergarten–Grade 2*. Reston, VA: National Council of Teachers of Mathematics.

Fosnot, C. T. (Ed.). (2010). *Models of Intervention in Mathematics: Reweaving the Tapestry*. Reston, VA: National Council of Teachers of Mathematics.

Kilpatrick, J., Swafford, J., & Findell, B. (Eds.). (2001). *Adding It Up*. Washington, D.C.: National Academy Press.

Kitchen, R. S., & Silver, E. A. (Eds.). (2010). *Assessing English Language Learners in Mathematics, A Research Monograph of TODOS: Mathematics for All*. Washington, D.C.: National Education Association.

Rathmell, E. C. (Ed.). (2011). *Developing Essential Understanding of Addition and Subtraction for Teaching Mathematics in Prekindergarten–Grade 2*. Reston, VA: National Council of Teachers of Mathematics.

Van De Walle, J., Karp, K., & Bay-Williams, J. (2010). *Elementary and Middle School Mathematics*. New York: Allyn & Bacon.

Standards Overview for *Math Games for the Common Core* (Grade 2)

Mathematical Content (Common Core State Standards for Grade 2)	2-1	2-2	2-3	2-4	2-5	2-6	2-7	2-8	2-9	2-10	2-11	2-12
Operations and Algebraic Thinking												
Add and subtract within 20. (2.OA.2)	✓	✓	✓									
Number and Operations in Base Ten												
Understand place value. (2.NBT.1–4)				✓	✓							
Use place value understandings and properties of operations to add and subtract. (2.NBT.5–9)				✓		✓	✓	✓	✓	✓	✓	✓
(CCSS) Standards for Mathematical Practice												
1. Make sense of problems and persevere in solving them.									✓	✓		
2. Reason abstractly and quantitatively.	✓		✓	✓	✓	✓	✓	✓	✓	✓	✓	✓
3. Construct viable arguments and critique the reasoning of others.				✓	✓	✓	✓	✓	✓	✓		
4. Model with mathematics.												
5. Use appropriate tools strategically.												
6. Attend to precision.							✓				✓	
7. Look for and make use of structure.	✓	✓				✓	✓				✓	✓
8. Look for and express regularity in repeated reasoning.				✓								

About the Authors

Gail Gerdemann is a retired teacher from the Corvallis School District in Oregon. She was also the Elementary Science Technology Engineering Math (STEM) Specialist for Oregon State University (1994–2012). Currently Gail is a consultant with several Oregon school districts.

Kathleen Barta is a retired teacher from North Clackamas School District in Oregon. She also was an instructor in Curriculum and Instruction for the University of Portland for many years. Currently Kathleen is Director of Teacher to Teacher Publications, Inc.

Special thanks to . . .

Linda Griffin, who was a major contributor to and reviewer of this project. She contributed many ideas, particularly for differentiation, and assisted the authors in making sure each unit was not only grounded in the Common Core State Standards but also in the research on which those standards were based. Linda is the Program Director for Early Childhood and Elementary Education at Lewis and Clark College, Portland, Oregon. Previously, she was the Mathematics Education Unit Director for the Northwest Regional Educational Laboratory.

Fast Facts

Learning Objectives

Focus on addition facts with numbers 6–9, and practice all facts within 20 for speed.

Content Standard

Fluently add and subtract within 20 using mental strategies. (CCSSM: 2.OA.2)

Prerequisite Skills

Students should be fluent, or nearly fluent, with adding within 10.

Math Vocabulary

decompose

sum

Materials

For each pair of students:	Warm-Up	"Fast Facts" Game
• Deck (2 sets) of Number Cards 0–10 (page 70)	✓	✓
• Ten-Frame Cards (page 58)	✓	✓
• Student-made "+" symbol cards		optional

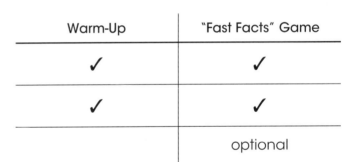

 Warm-Up A

Materials: · Deck (2 sets) of Number Cards 0–10 (page 70)
· Ten-Frame Cards for numbers 7, 8, and 9 (page 58)

Directions:

1. Students work with a partner. The partners sit side by side and take turns.

2. Place the Ten-Frame Card for 9 on the table between the two students.

3. A student draws one Number Card (for example, 6) to add to the 9.

4. Both students imagine a way to decompose 6 to make it easy to add to 9. For example, "Nine needs one more to make a 10, so if I take one from the 6, leaving 5, it's easy to add 10 and 5 to make 15."

5. The student says the sum and how he/she figured it out. (The student may use Ten-Frame Cards to help explain.) Then the student places the card that was drawn (6) in the discard pile.

6. The students repeat steps 1–3, but alternate which student starts. They continue until all the cards have been drawn.

 Warm-Up B

Directions:

1. Start with the Ten-Frame Card for 8.
2. Students follow the steps outlined above, but imagine how they could decompose the second number to make it easy to add to the 8.

 Warm-Up C

Directions:

Start with the Ten-Frame Card for 7. Students make their own visual strategy. (One strategy could include focusing on the fives structure. For example, with 6 + 7 a student might notice a full 5 in each addend and 1 + 2 extras.)

> *Note:* These warm-up exercises may be repeated as many times as needed.

⚲ Explaining the Game: Fast Facts

Number of Players: 2

Materials:

- Deck (2 sets) of Number Cards 0–10 (page 70)
- Ten-Frame Cards (page 58)
- 3 student-made "+" symbol cards for each player (optional)

  (*Note:* Some students may need to put a "+" symbol between the cards so they see the cards 8 and 7 as "8 + 7," not as "87.")

Object: Add two numbers to get the largest sum.

How to Play:

1. Each player draws two cards and mentally adds those numbers together.

2. The player says the sum.

3. If the sum is less than 11, the player draws another card. Repeat, as needed, until the sum is 11 or more.

4. The player with the larger sum wins all the cards.

5. If it is a tie, repeat steps 1–3, and the winner takes all the cards.

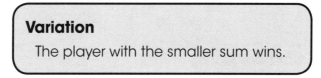

> **Variation**
>
> The player with the smaller sum wins.

(*Note:* Players may use Ten-Frame Cards to check their sums.)

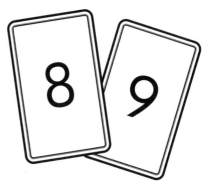

Differentiation

More Support

- Begin by substituting Ten-Frame Cards for Number Cards in the Warm-Up and game. When students are ready, use Number Cards.

- When using the Number Cards, have the Ten-Frame Cards available as a tool.

More Challenge (Above grade-level)

- Draw three Number Cards. Add the numbers together in any easy way. For example: 7 + 4 + 3 = (7 + 3) + 4 = 14. (*Note:* This challenge can encourage the use of the Commutative and Associative Properties.)

 Deepening the Understanding

Ask the class:	Mathematical Practices (CCSSM)
If you need to add 6 + 8, how could you think about the two addends to make the addition easier? Would you decompose either one, or is there another strategy that helps?	MP2 Reason abstractly and quantitatively. MP7 Look for and make use of structure.
Besides using ten-frames, how do you picture numbers in your head?	MP2 Reason abstractly and quantitatively.

What's the Difference?

Learning Objectives

Use a number line and mental strategies to find the difference between a number from 11 to 20 and a one-digit number.

Content Standard

Fluently add and subtract within 20 using mental strategies. (CCSSM: 2.OA.2)

Prerequisite Skills

Students should be fluent, or nearly fluent, with subtracting within 10 and adding within 20.

Math Vocabulary

difference
number line
subtraction

Materials

For each pair of students:

	Warm-Up	"What's the Difference?" Game
• Deck (2–4 sets) of Number Cards 1–10 (page 70)	✓	✓
• Deck (2 sets) of Number Cards 11–20 (page 71)		✓
• 0–20 Number Line (page 59)	✓	optional
• 2 paper clips	✓	optional

(*Note:* If you duplicate both sets of Number Cards, make sorting easy by using two different colors—for example, 1–10 in white and 11–20 in yellow.)

Warm-Up: Hidden Number

Number of Players: 2

Materials:

For each pair of students:
- Deck of Number Cards 1–9 (page 70)
- 0–20 Number Line (page 59)
- Paper clips

Object: Figure out the hidden number.

Directions:

1. The two players sit side by side and take turns.

2. Place the number line on the table between the two partners. Deal one card facedown and one card faceup.

3. Player 1:
   - Secretly looks at the facedown card.
   - Finds the sum of the two cards.
   - Says the sum.
   - Puts the paper clips on the number line to match the faceup card and the sum.

4. Player 2:
   - Figures out the hidden number.
   - Checks the answer by turning over the hidden card.

5. Now it's Player 2's turn to go first.

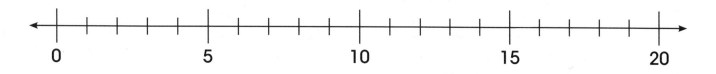

○ Explaining the Game: What's the Difference?

Number of Players: 2

Materials:

For each pair of students:

- Deck (2 or more sets) of Number Cards 1–10 (page 70)
- Deck (2 or more sets) of Number Cards 11–20 (page 71)
- Optional: 0–20 Number Line (page 59) and paper clips to mark the numbers on the number line

Object: Find the difference between two numbers.

How to Play:

1. Each player draws one card from each deck.

2. Each player mentally finds the difference between the two numbers.

3. The player with the larger difference wins those four cards.

4. If it is a tie, each player draws two more cards and repeats steps 2 and 3. The winner takes all eight cards.

⊞ Differentiation

"What's the Difference?" Game

More Support

- "Anchor" the larger number and play several rounds with that number. For example, from the 11–20 deck, Player 1 draws 16. Both players use 16 as the larger number for several rounds. For each round, each player draws the second card from the single-digit deck.

- *Note:* Keeping one number fixed will allow students to see and use relationships between numbers as a strategy.

More Challenge

- Limit the 1–10 deck to just the numbers 6–9.

⭐ Deepening the Understanding

Ask the class:	Mathematical Practices (CCSSM)
Explain how you could use 10 on the number line to help you subtract 16 – 7. What is an addition equation you could write to represent this problem? (7 + ? = 16)	MP2 Reason abstractly and quantitatively. MP7 Look for and make use of structure.
Using the cards 1–10 and 11–20 in this game, which combinations have a difference of 10? (For example: 17 – 7 = 10; 18 – 8 = 10.) What pattern do you see in these combinations?	MP2 Reason abstractly and quantitatively. MP7 Look for and make use of structure.
What do all the problems in Set A have in common that Set B combinations don't have?	MP2 Reason abstractly and quantitatively. MP7 Look for and make use of structure.

Set A	Set B
12 – 7	18 – 5
13 – 6	16 – 4
15 – 8	19 – 7

What is another example for Set A?

What is another example for Set B?

What Number Do I Have?

Learning Objectives

Add and subtract fluently within 20.

Content Standard

Fluently add and subtract within 20 using mental strategies. By end of Grade 2, know from memory all sums of two one-digit numbers. (CCSSM: 2.OA.2)

Prerequisite Skills

Students need to be comfortable using a number line and other mental strategies to add and subtract within 20 (Games 2-1 and 2-1).

Math Vocabulary

addend   equation

addition   fact families

difference   subtraction

General Vocabulary

English	Spanish
forehead	frente
salute	saludar

Materials

For each pair of students:

	Warm-Up A	Warm-Up B	"What Number Do I Have?" Game
• Deck (4 sets) of Number Cards 4–10 (page 70)	✓		
• Deck (2 sets) of Number Cards 11–18 (page 71)	✓		
• Fact Families Mat (page 60)	✓		
• Deck (4 sets) of Number Cards 0–9 (page 70)		✓	✓

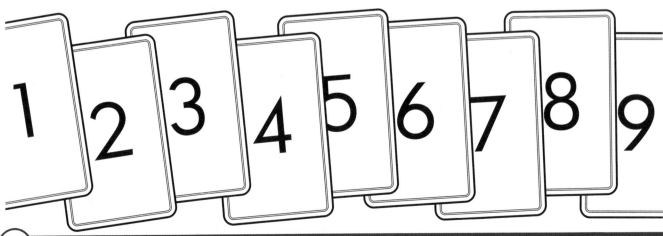

Warm-Up A: Fact Families

Number of Players: 2

Materials:

For each student:
- Deck (4 sets) of Number Cards 4–10 (page 70)
- Deck (2 sets) of Number Cards 11–18 (page 71)
- Fact Families Mat (page 60)

Object: Win sets of three cards by making addition and subtraction fact families.

Directions:

1. The two players sit side by side and take turns.

2. Deal five cards from the 4–10 deck to each player.

3. Turn over four cards from the 11–18 deck; place them between the players.

4. Taking turns, players:

   - Use two cards from their hand and one of the 11–18 cards to make an addition equation.

   - Place the three cards on the Fact Families Mat to show the addition equation.

   - Rearrange the cards to make a subtraction equation on the mat.

   - Then place those three cards in their "win pile."

5. Draw two new cards from the 4–10 deck to replace the two cards played.

6. Turn over another card from the 11–18 deck and place it between the players.

7. If no addition equation can be made, player may do an exchange by drawing one more card from the 4–9 deck and placing one card from his/her hand at the bottom of the deck.

8. If the player can make an addition equation with the new card, he/she may do that. If not, it is the other player's turn.

9. After the last card is drawn from the deck, each player gets one more turn to play. The winner is the player with the most cards.

Warm-Up B: Hidden Number

Number of Players: 2

Materials:

For each pair of students:

- Deck of Number Cards 0–9 (page 70)

Object: Figure out the hidden number.

Directions:

1. The two players sit side by side and take turns.

2. Player 1:
   - Draws two cards and places one card facedown and one card faceup.
   - Secretly looks at the facedown card.
   - Finds the sum of the two cards.
   - Says the sum.

3. Player 2:
   - Figures out the hidden number.

4. Now it's Player 2's turn to go first.

◯ Explaining the Game: What Number Do I Have?

Number of Players: 3 (1 "captain" and 2 "crewmembers")

Materials:

Deck of Number Cards 0–9 (page 70)

Object: Figure out the unseen number on your forehead by seeing your partner's number and knowing the sum of the two numbers.

How to Play:

1. The captain says, "Salute," and each player:
   - Draws a card.
   - Without looking at the card, puts it on his/her forehead so others can see it.

2. The captain says and writes the sum.

3. Cards stay on foreheads while each player figures out his/her own number.

4. The first player to correctly figure out his/her own number wins one point.

Differentiation

"What Number Do I Have?" Game

More Support

- Provide visual supports such as the 0–20 Number Lines (page 59) or Ten-Frame Cards (page 58), and/or

- First use a deck of Number Cards 0–5 or 0–6. Then add one more digit at a time.

More Challenge

- Use Number Cards 4–9 only.

- Use Number Cards 0–9 or 4–9. Play the game with groups of four students: 1 captain, 3 crewmembers—each with one addend. (Above grade level)

Deepening the Understanding

Ask the class:	Mathematical Practices (CCSSM)	
If your partner has "3" and the sum is "7," what is your number? How do you know? (Use math terms.) *What are all the different equations that could represent this?*	MP2	Reason abstractly and quantitatively.
	MP6	Attend to precision.
If your partner has "5" and the sum is "13," what is your number? How do you know? (Use math terms.) *What are all the different equations that could represent this?*	MP2	Reason abstractly and quantitatively.
	MP6	Attend to precision.
Could we play this game using subtraction as the "captain's" operation? What new rules or adjustments would we need to make in this new game?	MP2	Reason abstractly and quantitatively.

Skipping Around

Learning Objectives

Count to 1000; skip-count by 10s and 100s. (*Note:* These oral games are fast.)

Content Standards

Count within 1000; skip-count by . . . 10s, and 100s. (CCSSM: 2.NBT.2)

Mentally add 10 and 100 to a given number 100–900, and mentally subtract 10 or 100 from a given number 100–900. (CCSSM: 2.NBT.8)

Prerequisite Skills

Students should be proficient at counting by ones to 120, a Grade 1 standard.

Math Vocabulary

century
counting by:
    – ones
    – tens
    – hundreds
millennium
skip-counting

Materials

For each pair of students:

	Warm-Ups A and B	"Counting and Skipping" Game
• Deck (4 sets) of Number Cards 0–9 (page 70)	✓	✓
• Spinner (page 61)		✓

Pre-Warm-Up: Count by 10s and 100s

- Count by tens. Start with a two-digit number such as 64.
- Count by hundreds. Start with a three-digit number such as 371.

Warm-Up A: Entering a New Millennium

Number of Players: 2

Materials:

- Deck of Number Cards 0–9 (page 70)

Object: Be the first to "enter the new millennium," counting by hundreds.

Directions:

1. Player 1:
   - Turns over three number cards.
   - Makes the smallest possible three-digit number (for example, 206).
   - Says the number.

2. Player 2 says the next number, counting by 100s (for example, 306).

3. Player 3 says the next number, counting by 100s (for example, 406).

4. Players continue counting by 100s. (Examples: 506, 606, 706)

5. The player who goes over 1,000 or "enters the new millennium" wins a point.

6. For additional rounds, take turns being Player 1. Repeat Steps 1–5.

Notes:

- Zero may not be used as the leading digit in these games.
- Students are not required to count above 1,000. They may just say, "Entering the new millennium!"

🔌 Warm-Up B: Entering a New Century

Number of Players: 3–4

Materials:

- Deck of Number Cards 0–9 (page 70)

Object: Be the first to "enter a new century," counting by tens.

Directions:

1. Player 1:

   - Turns over three number cards to make the smallest possible three-digit number. (Zero may not be used in the hundreds place.)

   - Says the number (for example, 347).

2. Player 2 says the next number, counting by tens (for example, 357).

3. Players continue counting by tens. (Example: 367, 377, 387 …)

4. The player who says the number "in the new century" wins a point. (For this example, the player who says, "407" is the winner.)

Explaining the Game: Skipping Around (with Addition)

Number of Players: 3–4

Materials:

For each pair of students:
- Deck (4 sets) of Number Cards 0–9 (page 70)
- Spinner (page 61)

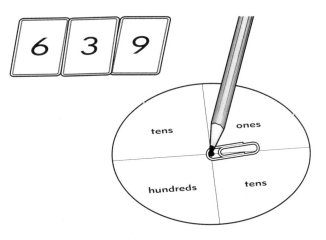

Object: Be the first to get to the next goal by counting or by skip-counting.

How to Play:

Optional: To make a record of play, keep a written list of the start number and skip-counted numbers.

1. Player 1 turns over three cards to make a three-digit "start number." (Zero may not be used in the hundreds place.)

2. Player 2 spins to determine the goal of the round. If the spinner lands on:
   - "Ones," player counts by ones until there is a new number in the tens place.
   - "Tens," player skip-counts by tens until a new number is in the hundreds place.
   - "Hundreds," player skip-counts by hundreds until there is a number over 1,000.

3. Players take turns saying the next number.

4. The first player to reach the goal wins that round.

5. For additional rounds, take turns being Player 1. Repeat steps 1–3.

Explaining the Game: Skipping Around (with Subtraction)

How to Play:

Use the same "Skipping Around" rules as above, except count backward by ones, tens, or hundreds. When skip-counting backward, continue to the smallest possible number that is larger than zero.

Differentiation

"Skipping Around" Game

More Support

- Begin with more skill building. For example:
  - Start at 10. Count by 10s to 100.
  - Start with 15. Count by 10s to 100.
  - Start at 100. Count by 100s to 1,000.
  - Start with 125. Count by 100s to 1,000.
- Allow students to use a number line or number grid.

More Challenge
(above Grade 2 standards)

- Change the spinner. Cross off one of the "tens" sections and write in "thousands." If the spinner lands on thousands, the goal is to count by thousands until there is a number that is over 10,000.

Deepening the Understanding

Ask the class:	Mathematical Practices (CCSSM)	
In the Millennium Game (Warm-Up A), if you start with 329, what is a quick way to predict the number of turns it will take to "enter a new millennium"?	MP2	Reason abstractly and quantitatively.
	MP6	Attend to precision.
	MP7	Look for and make use of structure.
If you start with 574, and count by tens, what is the winning number? (604) If you start with 383, and count by ones, what is the winning number? (390) If you start with 127, and count by hundreds, what is the winning number? (1,027) What do you notice about these three winning numbers? What do you notice about the position of the zero?	MP2	Reason abstractly and quantitatively.
	MP6	Attend to precision.
	MP7	Look for and make use of structure.
	MP8	Look for and express regularity in repeated reasoning.
If you start with 574, and count backward by tens, what is the winning number? (494)	MP2	Reason abstractly and quantitatively.
	MP6	Attend to precision.
	MP7	Look for and make use of structure.
Note: After a student shares an idea, ask the class if they agree or disagree. Why? Why not?	MP3	Construct viable arguments and critique the reasoning of others.

Everything Has Its Place

Learning Objectives

- Connect place value words and quantities with written three-digit numbers.
- Compare three-digit numbers based on meanings of hundreds, tens, and ones digits.
- Use symbols (<, >, =) in an analytical game.

Content Standards

Understand that the three digits of a three-digit number represent amounts of hundreds, tens, and ones; e.g., 706 equals 7 hundreds, 0 tens, and 6 ones . . . (CCSSM: 2.NBT.1)

    a. 100 can be thought of as a bundle of ten tens – called a "hundred."

    b. The numbers 100, 200, 300, . . . , 900 refer to one, two, three, . . . , nine hundreds (and 0 tens and 0 ones).

Compare two three-digit numbers based on meanings of hundreds, tens, and ones digits. Record results with symbols (<, >, =). (CCSSM: 2.NBT.4)

Prerequisite Skills

Students need an understanding of place value with two-digit numbers.

Math Vocabulary

comparison symbol (<, >, =)	place value
digit	ones place
equal	tens place
greater than	hundreds place
less than	

Materials

For each pair of students:	Warm-Up A	Warm-Up B	"Everything Has Its Place" Game
• Deck (4 sets) of Number Cards 0–10 (page 70)	✓		
• Place Value Word Cards: Hundreds, Tens, Ones (page 62)	✓		
• Warm-Up A Recording Sheet (page 63)	✓		
• Coin to flip	✓		
• Tiles or chips		✓	✓
• Student-made symbol cards (+ and –)		✓	
• Place Value Frames (page 64) – one per player		✓	
• Deck (4 sets) of Number Cards 0–9 (page 70)		✓	✓
• Student-made symbol cards (>, =)			✓
• Student-made place value mat			✓

🔌 Warm-Up A: Put Numbers in Their Place

Number of Players: 2

Materials:

For each pair of students:

- Deck of Number Cards 0–10 (page 70)
- 3 Place Value Word Cards: *hundreds*, *tens*, and *ones* (page 62)
- Coin to flip

For each student:

- Warm-Up A Recording Sheet (page 63)

Object: Create a three-digit numbers to match word and number cards.

Directions:

1. Each player:

    a. Turns over one place value card (*hundreds*, *tens*, or *ones*).

    b. Draws one number card and writes the value of hundreds, tens, or ones on the recording sheet.

    c. Reads his/her final number out loud.

    Example:

Number	Place Value Word Card	Value of the Cards
5	hundreds	500
9	ones	9
10	tens	100
	Total:	**609**

2. Flip a coin to determine the winner (heads: larger number wins; tails: smaller number wins).

3. Shuffle cards and play again.

🔌 Warm-Up B: Frame It!

Number of Players: 2

Materials:

For each pair of students:

- Deck (4 sets) of Number Cards 0–9 (page 70)
- Tiles or chips to represent points for winning
- Student-made (+/–) cards
- Place Value Frames for each player (page 64)

Object: Make a three-digit number that best matches the goal.

Directions:

Each player:

1. Draws three Number Cards and arranges the cards in his/her place value frame to make the largest possible three-digit number. (Zero may not be the leading digit.)

   For example, if the player draws Number Cards 3, 4, and 0:

   - Smallest is 304

3	0	0
	0	0
+		4
3	0	4

   - Largest is 430

4	0	0
	3	0
+		0
4	3	0

   - Other possible numbers are: 304, 340, 403, 430. The numbers 034 and 043 are not possible because zero cannot be the leading digit.

2. Reads his/her three-digit number out loud. (Read 532 as "five hundred thirty-two.") The player with the larger number wins.

3. Then, rearranges the same cards to create the smallest possible three-digit number on his/her place value frame.

4. Reads his/her three-digit number out loud. The player with the smaller number wins.

5. Repeat for additional rounds.

Explaining the Game: Everything Has Its Place

Number of Players: 2

Materials:

- Deck (4 sets) of Number Cards 0–9 for each pair of students (page 70)
- Index card with ">" on one side and "=" on the other side (*Note:* Turn the "<" symbol to indicate "<" or ">.")
- Tiles or chips to represent points for winning
- Place Value Mat (student-made)
  - ~ Cut 8.5 by 11-inch paper in half lengthwise to make a mat for each player. Use larger paper for standard playing cards.
  - ~ Fold each half in three sections, like a letter. Label each section.

Hundreds	Tens	Ones

Object: Create the largest three-digit number with three cards and correctly compare it to another three-digit number.

How to Play:

1. Taking turns, players draw four cards, one card at a time.

2. Players try to create the largest possible three-digit number by placing the card in one of the place value columns on their place value mat.

3. Once a card is placed, it cannot be moved.

4. When the 4th card is drawn, a player may:
   - Choose to replace one of the cards on the place value mat with it, or
   - Discard it.

5. The player with the larger three-digit number wins a point and:
   - Places a comparison symbol (<, >, =) between the numbers.
   - Reads the comparison statement (for example, 643 > 541)
   - Explains how he/she knows the winning number is larger.

6. Repeat steps 1–3. Play as many rounds as possible.

Variation

- Play for the smallest three-digit number.

Differentiation

Warm-Up A: "Put Numbers in Their Place"

More Support Version

- Begin by playing the game with Number Cards 0–9. When Number Card 10 is introduced, allow the use of base ten blocks.

More Challenge Version

- Repeat steps 1 and 2 until:
  - ~ One player's total is over 1,000,
    or
  - ~ Six Place Value Cards have been drawn.

"Everything Has Its Place" Game

More Support

- Begin by comparing two-digit numbers.

- Each player draws three cards and arranges them to make the largest or the smallest number. Then partners compare their numbers.

More Challenge (Above grade level)

- Adapt the game to include thousands
  - ~ Create a place value mat that includes thousands.
  - ~ When the fifth card is drawn, use it to replace a card or discard it.

Deepening the Understanding

Ask the class:	Mathematical Practices (CCSSM)
If you compare two three-digit numbers, how can you tell which is the larger? Use math terms. Explain why your comparing rule works.	MP2 Reason abstractly and quantitatively. MP6 Attend to precision. MP7 Look for and make use of structure.
After a student shares an idea, ask the class if they agree or disagree and why.	MP3 Construct viable arguments and critique the reasoning of others.

Visiting Tens – Addition

Learning Objectives

Sharpen mental math skills for adding within 100. Use the "make a ten" strategy and open number lines to add two-digit and one-digit numbers.

Content Standard

Fluently add … within 100, using … strategies based on place value … (CCSSM: 2.NBT.5)

Prerequisite Skills

- Students need to be fluent, or nearly fluent, with addition facts within 20 (Games 2–1 and 2–3) and skip-counting (Game 2–4), and also have a solid understanding of place value (Game 2–5).

Math Vocabulary

decompose

multiples of ten

open number line

sum

Materials

For each pair of students:

	Warm-Up	"Visiting Tens" Game
Deck (4 sets) of Number Cards 1–9 (page 70)	✓	✓
5–9 Spinner (page 72)	✓	
Markers – one color for each player	✓	
Hundred Chart (page 73) – optional		✓

To use the spinner, place a pencil tip through a paper clip.

Warm-Up: Jump to Cross 100

Number of Players: 2

Materials:

For each pair of students:

- Deck (4 sets) of Number Cards 1–9 (page 70)
- Markers – one color for each player
- 5–9 Spinner (page 72)
- Student-made open number line

Object: Use an open number line. Be the first whose sum is more than 100.

(*Note:* For the first round or two, some students may find it helpful to mark the multiples of 10 on the number line.)

Directions:

1. Player 1 draws two cards to make the smallest possible two-digit start number and then marks that number on the number line with his/her own marker.

2. Players take turns spinning and showing the addition of the "spinner number" to the last number on the number line. When possible, players show jumps that land on multiples of ten.

Example:

"Jump numbers" go on top.

Number line numbers go on the bottom.

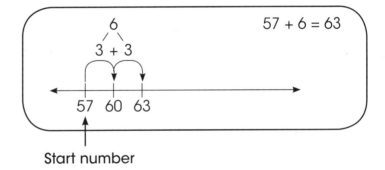

3. The winner is the first player to cross over 100 on the number line.

◯ Explaining the Game: Visiting Tens – Addition

Number of Players: 2

Materials:

- Deck (4 sets) of Number Cards 1–9 (page 70) – half for each player

Object: Win the most cards by adding numbers correctly and quickly.

How to Play:

1. Use one card from each player's deck to make a two-digit start number for each round.

2. Players take turns quietly saying, "1, 2, 3, go." Then each player draws another card from his/her own deck and adds that number to the shared start number.

3. Each player says his/her own sum.

4. The first player to say the sum correctly wins all four cards.

5. If a player says an incorrect sum, the other player wins all four cards.

6. If both players say the correct sum at the same time, they turn the cards over and play another round. The winner takes all eight of the cards.

7. Play continues until all the cards in both decks are used. The player with the most cards wins.

8. Players may use a hundred chart or other tools to check their work after they give their answers.

Start number: 57

🏠 Differentiation

Warm-Up: "Jump to Cross 100"

> *More Support*
> - Allow students to mark a number line with the multiples of 10 until they are ready to use an open number line.
> - Allow the use of ten-frame cards to represent the spinner number to help students visualize how to decompose numbers.

"Visiting Tens – Addition" Game

> *More Support*
> - Play a preliminary game with two sets of digit cards for each player.
>
> **Object:** Win as many cards as possible.
>
> 1. Deal two cards to create the smallest start number.
>
> 2. Taking turns, players draw one Number Card and report the sum of the start number and their Number Card.
>   - If correct, the player keeps the card.
>   - If the other player notices an error, he/she gets that card.
>
> 3. Keep the same start number. Repeat Step 2 until the deck is used up.
>
> 4. Put the used start number cards in a discard pile. As needed, shuffle the discard pile and play again.
>
> 5. Keep playing until there are no more cards in the deck or discard pile. The player with the most cards wins.

> *More Challenge*
> - Play without a number line. (Keep the number line in your head.).
> - Draw three-digit start numbers (above grade level).

Deepening the Understanding

Ask the class:	Mathematical Practices (CCSSM)	
Explain how you could use jumps that visit multiples of 10 in your head to add . . . 36 + 8 26 + 7 37 + 9	MP2	Reason abstractly and quantitatively.
	MP6	Attend to precision.
	MP7	Look for and make use of structure.
After a student shares an idea, ask the class if they agree or disagree and why.	MP3	Construct viable arguments and critique the reasoning of others.

Visiting Tens – Subtraction

Learning Objectives

Sharpen mental math skills for subtracting within 100. Use the "make a ten" strategy and open number lines and to subtract one-digit numbers from two-digit numbers.

Content Standard

Fluently . . . subtract within 100, using . . . strategies based on place value . . . (CCSSM: 2.NBT.5)

Prerequisite Skills

* Students need to be fluent, or nearly fluent, with subtraction facts within 20 (Games 2-2 and 2-3) and skip-counting (Game 2-4), and also have a solid understanding of place value (Game 2-5). Students should also be able to fluently use strategies based on place value to add within 100 (Game 2-6).

Math Vocabulary

difference

Materials

For each pair of students:

	Warm-Up	"Visiting Tens" Game
Deck (4 sets) of Number Cards 1–9 (page 70)	✓	✓
5–9 Spinner (page 72)	✓	
Colored markers, different color for each player	✓	
Hundred Chart (page 73) – optional		✓

To use the spinner, place a pencil tip through a paper clip.

Warm-Up: Jump to Cross Zero

Number of Players: 2

Materials:

For each pair of students:

- Deck (4 sets) of Number Cards 1–9 (page 70)
- 5–9 Spinner (page 72)
- Colored markers, different color for each player
- Student-made open number line

Object: Use an open number line to subtract. Be the first player whose difference would go past (below) zero.

(*Note:* For the first round or two, some students may find it helpful to mark the multiples of 10 on the number line.)

Directions:

1. Player 1 draws two cards to make the smallest possible two-digit start number, and then marks that number on the number line with his/her own marker.

2. Players take turns spinning and showing how to subtract the spinner number from the last recorded number on the number line. Players must show jumps that land on multiples of 10.

Example:

"Jump numbers" go on top.

Number line numbers go on the bottom.

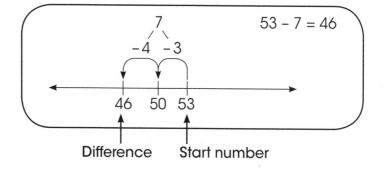

3. The winner's difference would go past (below) zero on the number line.

Explaining the Game: Visiting Tens – Subtraction

Number of Players: 2

Materials:

- Deck (4 sets) of Number Cards 1–9 (page 70) – half for each player

Object: Win the most cards by subtracting numbers correctly and quickly. Mental strategies, open number lines, or other written methods may be used.

How to Play:

1. Use one card from each player's deck to make a two-digit "start number" for each round.

2. Players take turns quietly saying, "1, 2, 3, go." Then each player draws another card from his/her own deck and subtracts that number from the shared "start number."

3. Each player says the answer to his/her problem.

4. The first player to say the difference correctly wins all four cards.

5. If a player is wrong, the other player wins all four cards.

6. If both players say the correct difference at the same time, they turn the cards over and play another round. The winner takes all eight of the cards.

7. Players may use a hundred chart or other tools to check their work after they give their answers.

8. Play continues until all the cards in both decks are used. The player with the most cards wins.

Start number: 53

🔲 Differentiation

Warm-Up: "Jump to Cross Zero"

> **⚙️**
>
> *More Support*
>
> - Allow students to mark a number line with multiples of 10 as long as they need to do that.
> - Encourage the use of ten-frame cards to represent the spinner number to help students visualize how to decompose numbers.

"Visiting Tens – Subtraction" Game

> **⚙️**
>
> *More Support*
>
> - Play a preliminary game with a small deck (2 sets) of Number Cards 1–9. The object is to win as many cards as possible.
>
> **How to Play:**
>
> 1. Draw two cards to create the smallest possible "start number."
> 2. Take turns drawing one card and subtracting the number on that card from the "start number."
>   - If correct, put your number card in a "win pile."
>   - If the other player notices an error, he/she wins that card.
>   - Keep the same start number. Repeat Step 2 until the deck is used up.
> 3. The winner is the player who has the most cards in his/her "win pile."

> **♜**
>
> *More Challenge*
>
> - Draw three-digit "start numbers." (Above grade level)

Deepening the Understanding

Ask the class:	Mathematical Practices (CCSSM)	
Explain how you could use jumps that visit multiples of 10 in your head to subtract . . . 56 – 8, 64 – 7	MP2	Reason abstractly and quantitatively.
	MP6	Attend to precision.
What is a general rule for doing this process in your head?	MP7	Look for and make use of structure.
After a student shares an idea, ask the class if they agree or disagree and why.	MP3	Construct viable arguments and critique the reasoning of others.

Chunks Make It Easy

Learning Objectives

Fluently add and subtract numbers with sums within 100.

Add and subtract multiples of 10 to numbers within 1,000, and subtract multiples of 10 from numbers within 1,000, using mental math strategies based on place value and open number lines.

Content Standard

Fluently add and subtract within 100, using strategies based on place value, properties of operations … (CCSSM: 2.NBT.5)

Add and subtract within 1000, using concrete models or drawings and strategies based on place value … (CCSSM: 2.NBT.7)

Prerequisite Skills

Students should be able to:

- Fluently add and subtract numbers with sums to 20 (Games 2-1, 2-2, and 2-3).
- Be familiar with using open number lines for addition and subtraction (Games 2-6 and 2-7).

Math Vocabulary

sum

difference

Materials

For each pair of students:

	Warm-Ups A and B	"Chunks Make It Easy" Games (+/–)
Deck (4 sets) of Number Cards 1–9 (page 70)	✓	✓
Spinner for Warm-Ups A and B (page 65)	✓	
Spinner for "Chunks Make It Easy" Game (page 66)		✓
"Chunks Make It Easy" Recording Sheet (page 67)		as needed

⚡ Warm-Up A: Keep On Adding to 1,000

Materials:

For each pair of students:
- Deck of Number Cards 1–9 (page 70)
- Warm-Up Spinner (page 65)

Object: Be the first player whose sum is over 1,000.

Directions:

1. Player 1 draws three cards to make a "start number" between 400 and 800 and begins a list with that number.

2. Player 2 spins for a number to add, then adds the "spinner number" to the "start number" and writes that sum on the list.

3. Players take turns spinning, adding the "spinner number" to the last number on the list, and writing the new sum on the list.

4. The winner is the player whose sum is greater than 1,000.

> **Example of a list:**
>
> | | |
> |---|---|
> | Start number: | 632 |
> | Spinner number 70: | 702 |
> | Spinner number 80: | 782 … and so on |

⚡ Warm-Up B: Keep On Trekking to 300

Materials:

The same as for Warm-Up A

Object: Be the first player whose difference is less than 300.

Directions:

1. Use the same rules as the "Adding to 1,000" game, but players subtract the spinner number.

2. The winner is the first player whose difference is less than 300

**Spinner for Warm-Ups
A and B**

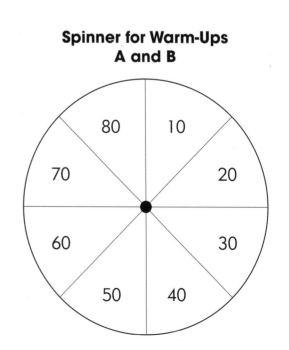

◯ Explaining the Game: Chunks Make It Easy – Addition

Number of Players: 2

Materials:

- Deck (4 sets) of Number Cards 1–9 (page 70)
- Game Spinner (page 66)

Object: Win the most cards by adding sums correctly and saying the sum quickly.

How to Play:

1. Each player turns over two cards and makes the smallest possible two-digit "start number."

2. Player 1 quietly says, "1, 2, 3, go," and then spins the spinner.

3. Each player mentally adds that spinner number to his/her own "start number."

4. The first player to say the sum correctly wins all four "start number" cards:

   - Each player must say his/her own sum.
   - If a player says an incorrect sum, the other player wins all four cards.

5. If both players say the correct sum at the same time, they turn the cards over and play again. The winner takes all eight of those cards.

6. Players may check sums by using an open number line, hundred chart, or other tools.

7. Players play additional rounds until the deck is used up. The player with the most cards wins the game.

"Chunks Make It Easy" Spinner

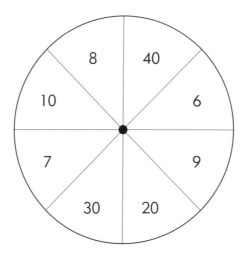

Explaining the Game: Chunks Make It Easy – Addition

(A Less Competitive Variation)

Number of Players: 2

Materials:

- Deck (4 sets) of Number Cards 1–9 (page 70)
- Game Spinner (page 66)

Object: Win the most cards by adding numbers correctly and saying the sum quickly.

How to Play:

1. Deal two cards to create the smallest possible two-digit "start number."

2. Taking turns, players spin the spinner and quickly report the sum of the "start number" and the "spinner number" using mental math strategies.

3. If correct, the player keeps his/her two "start number" cards. If incorrect, the other player gets the two cards.

4. Play continues until there are no more cards in the deck. The player with the most cards is the winner.

Explaining the Game: Chunks Make It Easy – Subtraction

Object: Win the most cards by subtracting numbers correctly and saying the difference quickly.

How to Play:

Use the same materials and rules as the "Chunks Make It Easy – Addition" game except players:

1. Make the largest possible "start number."

2. Find the difference between the "spinner number" and their own "start number." Subtract the smaller number from the larger number. Say out loud the difference between the two numbers.

Differentiation

"Match the Fraction" Game

More Support

- Use the "Chunks Make It Easy" Recording Sheet (page 67).

Starting Number	Spinner Number	Sum
27	⑨ 3 + 6	36
㊺ 40 + 5	30	75
61	8	69

More Challenge

- Use two spinners. Players must add both of the spinner numbers to their "start number." For example, if the "start number" is 38 and one spinner shows 30 and the other shows 7, the player must find the sum of all three numbers: 38 + 30 + 7 = 75.

 # Deepening the Understanding

Ask the class:	Mathematical Practices (CCSSM)
Use a mental math strategy or an open number line. For each sum, explain how you could decompose one of the two addends to make adding easier. 27 + 6 =　　48 + 7 =　　356 + 8 = 27 + 60 =　　86 + 70 =　　356 + 80 =	MP2　Reason abstractly and quantitatively.
Use a mental math strategy or an open number line. For each sum, explain how you could decompose one of the two addends to make adding easier. 52 – 3 =　　63 – 5 =　　356 – 8 = 52 – 30 =　　63 – 50 =　　356 – 80 =	MP2　Reason abstractly and quantitatively.
After a student shares an idea, ask the class if they agree or disagree and why.	MP3　Construct viable arguments and critique the reasoning of others.

Three in Any Row – Addition

Learning Objectives

Add one-digit plus two-digit numbers and two-digit plus two-digit numbers in a game that requires attention to place value.

Content Standard

Fluently add . . . within 100, using strategies based on place value . . . (CCSSM: 2.NBT.5)

Prerequisite Skills

Students should have experience using an open number line and mental strategies for adding one- and two-digit numbers within 100 (Games 2-4 and 2-6).

Math Vocabulary

diagonal   subtract

difference   vertical

horizontal

General Vocabulary

English	Spanish
capture	capturar

Materials

For each pair of students:

	Warm-Up	"Three in Any Row (+)" Game
• Deck of Number Cards 1–9 (page 70)	✓	✓
• Hundred Chart (game board) (page 73)		✓
• "Three in Any Row" Recording Sheet (page 74) – optional		✓
• "Compose and Decompose – Addition" Recording Sheet (page 68) – as needed		✓
• 2 colored markers		✓

Warm-Up: Get Past 100

Number of Players: 2

Materials:

For each pair of students:

- Deck of Number Cards 1–9 (page 70)

Object: Be the player whose sum would be more than 100.

Directions:

1. Player 1 draws two Number Cards to make a two-digit "start number" (for example, 57).

2. Player 1 records that number.

3. Player 2 draws two Number Cards and uses those cards to make a two-digit number (for example, 26).

4. Player 2 adds that number to the first number and records the sum.

5. Players take turns drawing cards and adding the new two-digit number to the last sum. Play continues until a player has a sum that is more than 100.

Example A: Using a Number Line

Player 1 marked the start number, 57.

Player 2 showed jumps of 10 + 10 + 3 + 3 to add 26 to the start number.

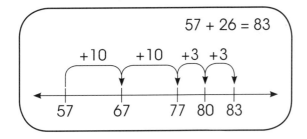

$$57 + 26 = 83$$

Example B: Using Decomposing and Composing

Player 1 writes: $57 = 50 + 7$

Player 2 writes: $26 = 20 + 6$

So, adding the tens and then the ones:

$50 + 20 = 70; 7 + 6 = 13$

$70 \quad + \quad 13 \quad = 83$

⬤ Explaining the Game: Three in Any Row – Addition

Number of Players: 2

Materials:

For each pair of students:

- Hundred Chart (game board) (page 73)
- Deck (4 sets) of Number Cards 1–9 (page 70)
- "Three in Any Row" Recording Sheet (page 74) – optional
- "Compose and Decompose" Recording Sheet (page 68) – as needed for differentiation
- 2 colored markers

Object: Capture three numbers in any row (horizontal, vertical, or diagonal) on the shared Hundred Chart (game board) by adding two 2-digit numbers. Numbers do not need to be adjacent to each other.

How to Play:

1. Taking turns, players:
   - Draw four cards.
   - Create two 2-digit numbers.
   - Add the two numbers and mark the sum on the game board.

2. If the numbers cannot be arranged so that the sum is between 1 and 100, player draws another card and discards one card. Repeats, if necessary.

3. To have a record of play, players write the equations on the Recording Sheet.

4. Play continues until one player captures three numbers in any row.

> **Advanced version:**
> Capture three or more adjacent numbers in a row (horizontal, vertical, or diagonal). Game may be played competitively or cooperatively.

1	2	3	4	5	6	7	8	9	10
11	12	13	14	15	16	17	18	19	20
21	22	23	24	25	26	27	28	29	30
31	32	33	34	35	36	37	38	39	40
41	42	43	44	45	46	47	48	49	50
51	52	53	54	55	56	57	58	59	60
61	62	63	64	65	66	67	68	69	70
71	72	73	74	75	76	77	78	79	80
81	82	83	84	85	86	87	88	89	90
91	92	93	94	95	96	97	98	99	100

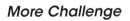 **Differentiation**

"Three in Any Row – Addition" Game

More Support

- Continue playing Warm-Up Exercise A, as needed, before playing the game.

- Use the "Compose and Decompose – Addition" Recording Sheet.

More Challenge

Play "The Target Number" Game

Number of Players: 2

Materials: Hundred Chart (game board)

Object: Create up to three different 2-digit plus 2-digit equations that equal the target number.

Rules

1. Toss a coin onto the Hundred Chart. Wherever it lands is the target number.

2. Each player writes three addition equations with two 2-digit numbers that equal the target number. For example, for the target number 57, three equations are:

$$19 + 38 = 57$$
$$42 + 15 = 57$$
$$27 + 30 = 57$$

3. Score one point for each unique digit used. For the example above, the score is 9 points for using nine digits: 0, 1, 2, 3, 4, 5, 7, 8, 9.

4. Toss a coin again for a new round.

⭐ Deepening the Understanding

Ask the class:	Mathematical Practices (CCSSM)
Explain how you could use composing and decomposing numbers to add these numbers in your head. $38 + 27 =$ $56 + 19 =$	**MP2** Reason abstractly and quantitatively.
Jan drew four cards: 3, 6, 1, and 8. She combined them in different ways to make two-digit numbers. • What are four different sums that Jenny could make? • For each of those sums, find one or more ways that you could create that sum by rearranging the cards. (If students do not generate all of these, you could add to their list.) $\quad\quad 13 + 68 = 81$ $\quad\quad 13 + 86 = 99$ $\quad\quad 16 + 38 = 54$ $\quad\quad 16 + 83 = 99$ $\quad\quad 18 + 36 = 54$ $\quad\quad 18 + 63 = 81$ $\quad\quad 31 + 68 = 99$ $\quad\quad 31 + 86 = 117$ $\quad\quad 36 + 81 = 117$	**MP1** Make sense of problems and persevere in solving them. **MP2** Reason abstractly and quantitatively.
After a student shares an idea, ask the class if they agree or disagree and why.	**MP3** Construct viable arguments and critique the reasoning of others.

Three In Any Row – Subtraction

Learning Objectives

Subtracts one- and two-digit numbers from two-digit numbers in a game that requires attention to place value.

Content Standard

Fluently add and subtract within 100, using strategies based on place value, properties of operations, and/or the relationship between addition and subtraction. (CCSSM: 2.NBT.5)

Prerequisite Skills

Students should have experience using an open number line and mental strategies for adding and subtracting one- and two-digit numbers within 100 (Games 2-6, 2-7, 2-8, and 2-9).

Math Vocabulary

diagonal

equation

horizontal

vertical

General Vocabulary

English	Spanish
capture	capturar

Materials

For each pair of students:	Warm-Up	"Three in Any Row (–)" Game
• Deck of Number Cards 0–9 (page 70)	✓	✓
• Hundred Chart (game board) (page 73)		✓
• Colored markers		✓
• "Three in Any Row" Recording Sheet (page 74) – optional		
• "Compose and Decompose – Subtraction" Recording Sheet – optional (page 69)		✓

🔌 Warm-Up: Subtract to Zero

Number of Players: 2

Materials:

For each pair of students:

- Deck of Number Cards 0–9 (page 70)

Object: Be the player whose difference would go below 0.

Directions:

1. Player 1 draws two Number Cards to make a two-digit "start number" and records the number.

2. Player 2 draws two more cards to make a two-digit number, subtracts that second number from the first number, and records the difference.

3. Play alternates until one player, the winner, has a difference that would go below zero.

4. Students may use any method of subtraction.

Example A: Using an open number line

Student 1 marks the start number, 57.

Student 2 shows jumps on the number line to subtract 27.

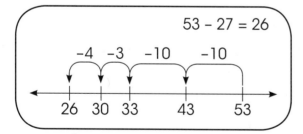

Example B: Using skip-counting and mental math

Student 1 writes 53.

Student 2 thinks, "53, 43, 33; 33 – 7 = 26."

Example C: Using decomposing and composing

Student 1 writes: 53 = 50 + 3

Student 2 writes: 27 = 20 + 7

Then they subtract first the tens and then the ones:

50 – 20 = 30; 3 – 7 = (Oops. Have to split up 53 more.)

53 = 40 + (10 + 3) or 40 + 13

Tens	Ones
40	13
– 20	– 7

20 + 6 = 26

Now it is Student 1's turn to draw two cards, make a number, and subtract it from 26.

⭕ Explaining the Game: Three in Any Row – Subtraction

Number of Players: 2

Materials:

- Hundred Chart (game board) (page 73)
- Deck (4 sets) of Number Cards 0–9 (page 70)
- Colored markers – a different color for each player
- "Three in Any Row" Recording Sheet (page 74) – optional

Object: Capture three numbers in any row (horizontal, vertical, or diagonal) on the shared Hundred Chart by subtracting numbers. Numbers do not need to be adjacent to each other.

Game Rules:

1. Taking turns, players:
   - Draw four cards.
   - Create a two-digit minus a two-digit problem, or
   - Make a two-digit minus a one-digit problem and discard the unused card.
   - Subtract the smaller number from the larger number and mark (capture) the difference on the game board.

2. Play continues until one player has captured three numbers in any row, column, or on the diagonal.

(*Note:* To have a record of play, players write the equations they create on the Recording Sheet.)

More Advanced Game

Use the same rules as above, but capture three adjacent numbers in any row (horizontal, vertical, or diagonal).

Differentiation

More Support

Play the "Three in Any Row – Subtraction" Game

- Continue playing the Warm-Up activity, as needed, before playing the game.

- Use the "Compose and Decompose – Subtraction" Recording Sheet.

More Challenge

Play the "Target Number" Game

Number of Players: 2

Materials: Hundred Chart (game board)

Object: Create up to three different 2-digit minus 2-digit equations that equal the target number. Score one point for each unique digit used.

Rules

1. Toss a coin onto the Hundred Chart. Wherever it lands is the target number.

2. Each player writes three different 2-digit minus 2-digit subtraction equations that equal the target number. Score one point for each unique digit used.

   Example for target number 29:

   $$42 - 13 = 29$$
   $$56 - 27 = 29$$
   $$80 - 51 = 29$$

   The score for these equations would be 10 points for the use of 10 different digits (0–9).

3. Toss a coin again for a new round.

⭐ Deepening the Understanding

Ask the class:	Mathematical Practices (CCSSM)
Explain how you could take numbers apart or put them together to subtract in your head or on an open number line. $\qquad$ $64 - 38 =$ $\qquad$ $73 - 49 =$	MP2 Reason abstractly and quantitatively.
Henry used the digits 3, 6, 1, and 8. He rearranged the digits in the tens and ones places to create different numbers with the same difference. $\qquad$ $86 - 31 = 55$ $\qquad$ $68 - 13 = 55$ $\qquad$ $63 - 18 = 45$ $\quad$ $36 - 81 \longrightarrow 81 - 36 = 45$ Henry thought this would work with any four digits. Do you agree? Why? Why not?	MP1 Make sense of problems and persevere in solving them. MP2 Reason abstractly and quantitatively.
After a student shares an idea, ask the class if they agree or disagree and why.	MP3 Construct viable arguments and critique the reasoning of others.

What's My Secret Number?

Learning Objectives

Use the relationship between addition and subtraction to find the missing addend.

Content Standard

Fluently add and subtract within 100, using strategies based on place value, properties of operations, and/or the relationship between addition and subtraction. (CCSSM: 2.NBT.5)

Explain why addition and subtraction strategies work, using place value and the properties of operations. (CCSSM: 2.NBT.9)

Prerequisite Skills

Students need to be fairly fluent with adding and subtracting within 100 (Games 2-9 and 2-10).

General Vocabulary

English	Spanish
captain	*capitán*
crewmember	*miembro de la tripulación*

Materials

For each pair of students:

	Warm-Up	"Secret Number" Game
• Deck of Number Cards 1–9 (page 70)	✓	✓
• Three privacy barriers (file folders, etc.)	✓	✓
• Sticky notes or other small notes	✓	✓
• Tiles	✓	✓
• Hundred Chart – optional (page 73)	✓	✓

⚡ Warm-Up

Play the same game as "What's My Secret Number?" (this page), but limit the card deck to numbers 1–5.

◯ Explaining the Game: What's My Secret Number?

Number of Players: 3 (1 captain and 2 crewmembers)

Materials:

For each team of 3 players:

- Deck of Number Cards 1–9 (page 70)
- Tiles or chips to represent winning points
- Hundred Chart – optional (page 73)

For each student:

- Privacy barrier
- Paper for open number lines or other written work
- Sticky notes or small notepaper

Object: Figure out your partner's "secret number" by subtracting or finding the missing addend.

> **Less Competitive Version:**
>
> Players have one minute to figure out the other crewmember's secret number. If both are correct and can show why, each gets a winning tile.

Directions:

1. Behind a privacy barrier, each crewmember writes his/her secret number on two sticky notes or notepaper (one to keep, one to give to the captain):
   - Crewmember 1 writes any two-digit number.
   - Crewmember 2 draws a Number Card and writes that number.

2. Each crewmember passes one of the notes to the captain.

3. The captain adds the two secret numbers and then says and writes the sum on paper so both crewmembers can see it. Paper and pencil or a hundred chart may be used.

4. Each crewmember figures out the other crewmember's secret number.

5. The first crewmember to correctly say the other crewmember's secret number is the winner, but to win a tile, s/he must show why the answer is correct.

6. Rotate the roles and play again.

▣ Differentiation

"What's My Secret Number?" Game

More Support ⚙

- Continue to play the Warm-Up game until students are comfortable.
- Gradually introduce additional numbers (6–9) to the deck.

More Challenge ♖

- The captain creates a third addend by writing a one-digit number on a sticky note and placing it on the table for all to see. Then play continues in the same way as before, but now includes a third number to add to the crewmembers' two secret numbers.

✦ Deepening the Understanding

Ask the class:	Mathematical Practices (CCSSM)
Show this number line: $$\overset{8}{\frown}$$ 57 65 What are all the equations that could be represented by this diagram? How do you know?	MP2 Reason abstractly and quantitatively. MP6 Attend to precision. MP7 Look for and make use of structure.
If the captain says the sum is 56 and your secret number is 47: • Write an equation to show how you would figure out the other player's secret number. • How could you check to see if you got the correct answer without peeking at the other player's secret number? (*Note:* Encourage the use of the relationship between addition and subtraction.)	MP2 Reason abstractly and quantitatively. MP6 Attend to precision. MP7 Look for and make use of structure.

It All Adds Up

Learning Objectives

Create an addition problem with three or four two-digit numbers to match the goal of largest sum or smallest sum.

Content Standard

Add up to four two-digit numbers using strategies based on place value and properties of operations. (CCSSM: 2.NBT.6)

Add and subtract within 1000, using concrete models or drawings and strategies based on place value, properties of operations, and/or the relationship between addition and subtraction . . . (CCSSM 2.NBT.7)

Prerequisite Skills

Students should be fluent with adding two numbers with sums within 100 (Game 2-9).

General Vocabulary

English	Spanish
row	hilera

Materials

For each pair of students:	Warm-Up	"It All Adds Up" Game
• Deck (4 sets) of Number Cards 1–9 (page 70)	✓	✓
• 1 set of Number Cards 11–20 (page 71)	✓	
• 4 student-made "+" signs – optional	✓	

⚡ Warm-Up: Three Little Addends

Number of Players: 2

Materials:

For each pair of students:

- Deck (4 sets) of Number Cards 1–9 (page 70)
- 1 set of Number Cards 11–20 (page 71)
- 4 student-made "+" signs – optional (*Note:* Some students may see the three addends—for example, 14, 6, and 8—as 14 + 68. The "+" signs can help students see 14 + 6 + 8.)

Object: Find the sum of three numbers.

Directions:

1. Each player:
   - Draws two cards from the 1–9 deck and one card from the 11–20 deck.
   - Adds his/her three addends.

2. The player with the larger sum wins all six cards.

3. If there is a tie, each player draws three more cards. The player with the larger sum wins all 12 cards.

> **Note:**
>
> This game may encourage students to use the Associative and Commutative Properties, although they are not expected to identify the use of those properties. Here are two easy mental strategies:
>
> - Combine the two smaller numbers and then add that sum to the larger number.
> - Start with the largest number (11–20) and then decide which of the other two numbers to add next.

Explaining the Game: It All Adds Up

Number of Players: 2

Materials:

- Deck (4 sets) of Number Cards 1–9 (page 70)

Object: Create an addition problem with three two-digit numbers to make a sum as close as possible to the target number.

—◄o►—

Game Rules for Cooperative Six-Card Game

1. Players are teammates.

2. Make a target number. Write 1 in the hundreds place. Then turn over a card for the tens place and a card for the ones place.

3. Players draw six cards to share. They use the cards to make three two-digit numbers with a sum as close as possible to the target number. (If the smallest possible sum would be over 1,000, player draws one more card and discards one card. Repeat, if necessary.)

4. The team score is the difference between the target number and the sum. (Subtract the smaller number from the larger number.)

—◄o►—

Game Rules for Competitive Six-Card Game

Use the same Game Rules as for the Cooperative Six-Card Game, except:

- Players are opponents.
- Each player draws six cards.
- The player with the sum closest to the target number wins.

—◄o►—

Eight-Card Version

Rules: Use the same Game Rules as for the Six-Card Games, but work with eight cards to create four two-digit addends.

Differentiation

"It All Adds Up" Game

More Support

- Play the Warm-Up game many times, until students are ready to try the "It All Adds Up" game.

- Choose the second single-digit card from a faceup set of Number Cards 5–10, rather than draw from a facedown deck. (The goal is to choose a "friendly" number to complement the first one, which was randomly drawn.)

More Challenge (above grade level)

- Draw 4 cards to create the smallest possible target number.

- Draw nine cards to create three 3-digit numbers.

- The player with the sum closest to the target number wins a point.

Deepening the Understanding

Ask the class:	Mathematical Practices (CCSSM)
Reynoldo accidentally ripped his paper, and all he can see are the tens digits in his addition problem:	MP2 Reason abstractly and quantitatively.
	MP6 Attend to precision.
	MP7 Look for and make use of structure.

$$
\begin{array}{r}
2\,\underline{} \\
1\,\underline{} \\
+\,4\,\underline{} \\
\hline
\end{array}
$$

Which of the following are possible right answers? Explain and give example(s) to support your reasoning.

66

76

86

96

106

Blackline Masters

ACTIVITY-SPECIFIC REPRODUCIBLES

REPRODUCIBLES USED IN MORE THAN ONE GAME

GAME RULES

Ten-Frame Cards (Game 2-1)

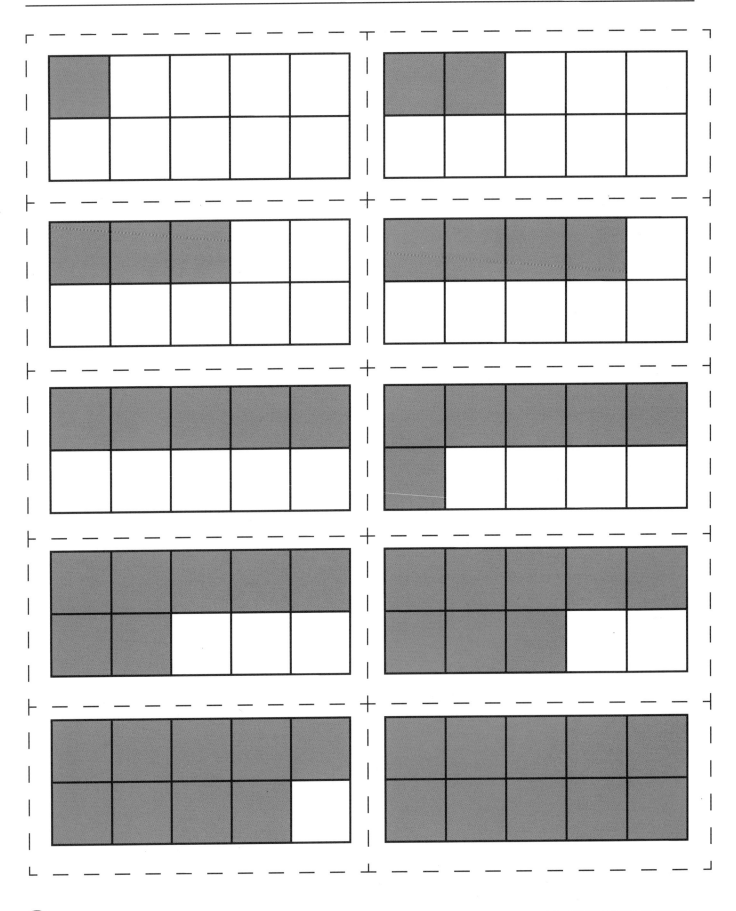

Math Games for the Common Core   © Didax — www.didax.com

0 to 20 Number Lines (Game 2-2)

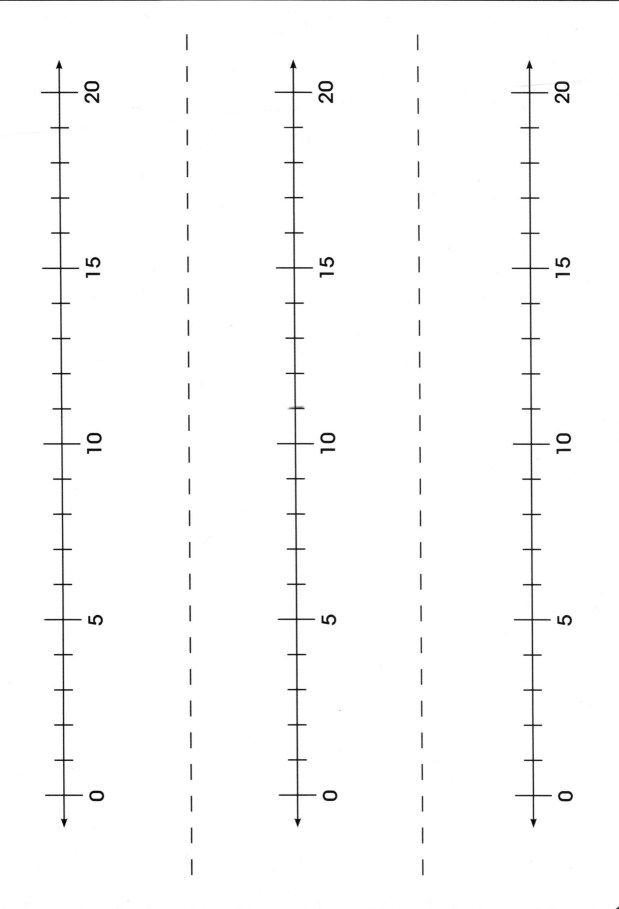

Fact Families Mat (Game 2-3)

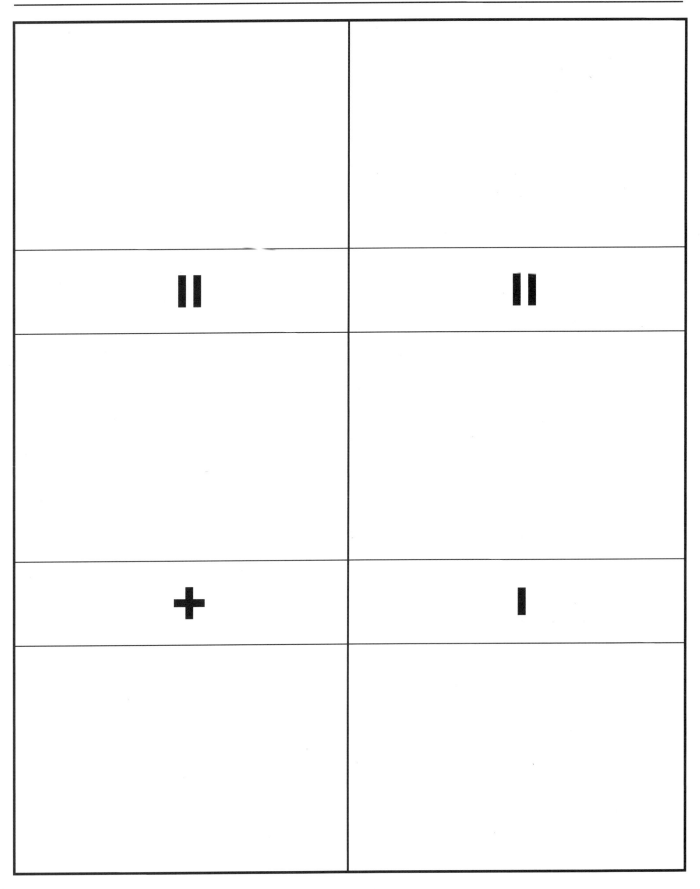

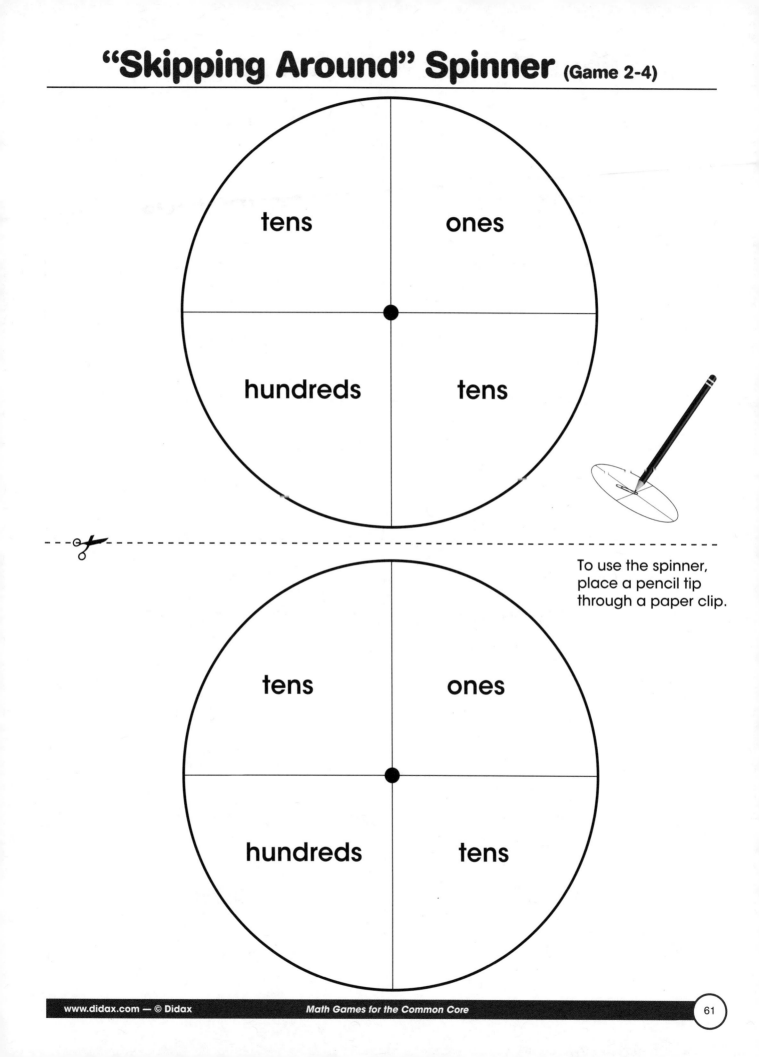

To use the spinner, place a pencil tip through a paper clip.

Place Value Word Cards (Game 2-5)

hundreds	hundreds
tens	tens
ones	ones
hundreds	hundreds
tens	tens
ones	ones

"Everything Has . . ." Warm-Up A
Recording Sheet (Game 2-5)

Example:

h = hundreds

t = tens

o = ones

Number	Place Value Word Card	Value of the Cards
5	h	500
9	o	9
10	t	100
	Total:	609

Number	Place Value Word Card	Value of the Cards
	Total:	

Number	Place Value Word Card	Value of the Cards
	Total:	

Number	Place Value Word Card	Value of the Cards
	Total:	

Place Value Frame (Game 2-5)

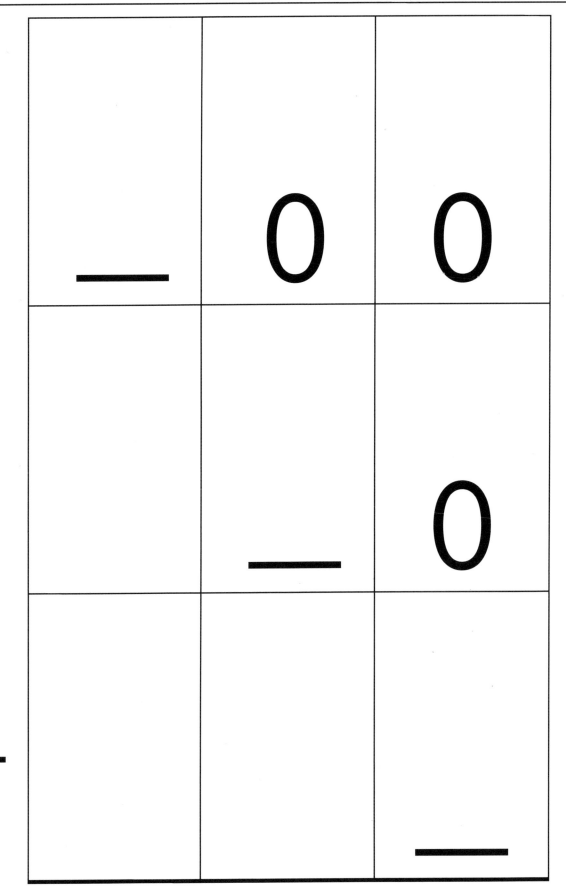

"Chunks Make It Easy" Warm-Up Spinners (Game 2-8)

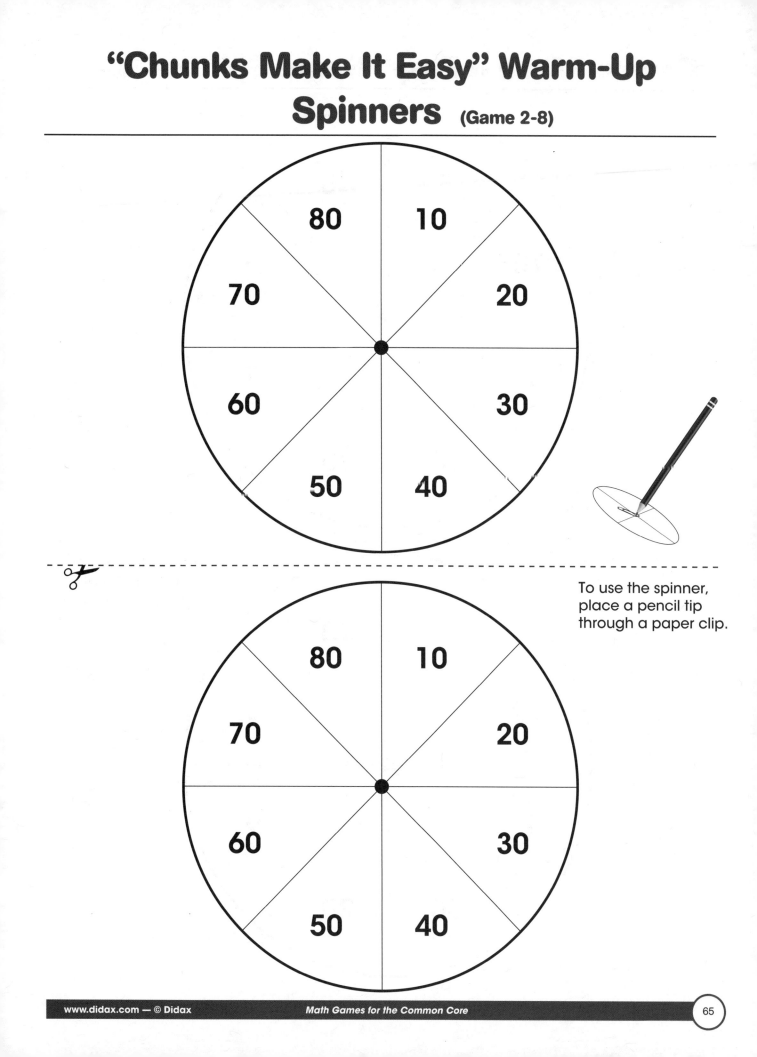

To use the spinner, place a pencil tip through a paper clip.

"Chunks Make It Easy" Game Spinner (Game 2-8)

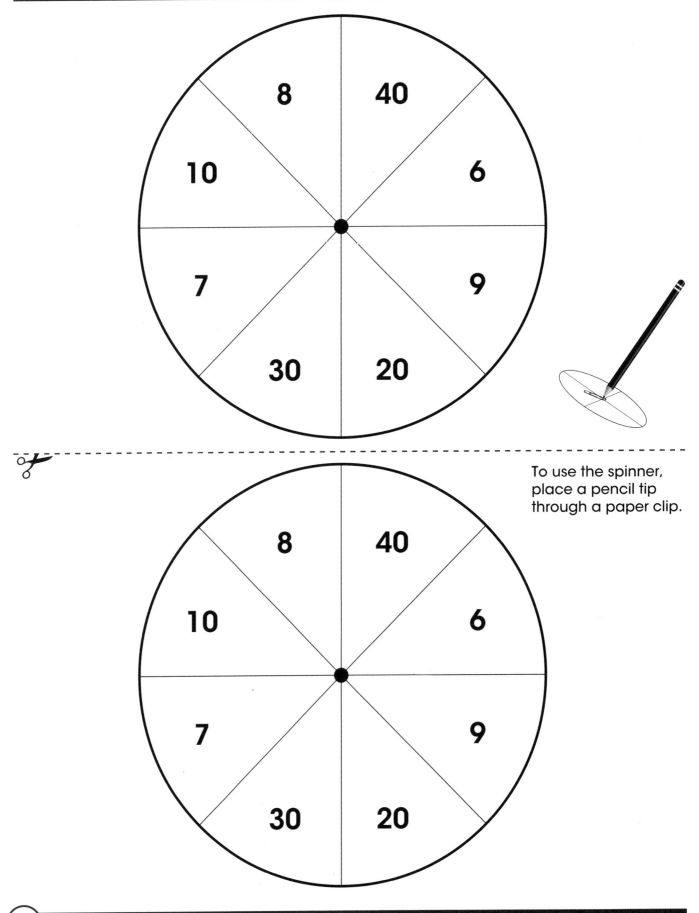

To use the spinner, place a pencil tip through a paper clip.

"Chunks Make It Easy"
Recording Sheet (Game 2-8)

Name: _____

How I added or subtracted:

Start Number	Spinner Number	Sum or Difference

"Compose and Decompose – Addition"
Recording Sheet (Game 2-9)

Player 1: _____

The Problem	Show How You Compose and Decompose the Numbers				
$\begin{array}{r} 56 \\ +27 \\ \hline \end{array}$	One way: $\begin{array}{r} 50 + 6 \\ 20 + 7 \\ \hline 70 + 13 = 83 \end{array}$				

Player 2: _____

The Problem	Show How You Compose and Decompose the Numbers				

"Compose and Decompose – Subtraction" Recording Sheet (Game 2-10)

Player 1: _____

The Problem	Show How You Compose and Decompose the Numbers
53 − 27	One way: 53 = 40 + 13 40 13 27 = 20 + 7 −20 −7 20 + 6 = 26

Player 2: _____

The Problem	Show How You Compose and Decompose the Numbers

Number Cards 0–10

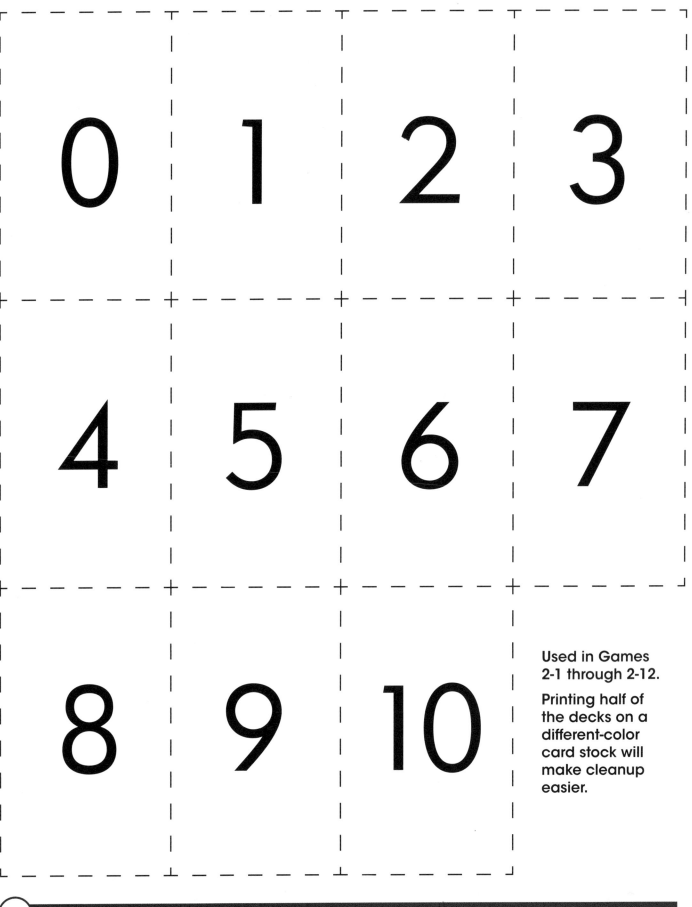

0   1   2   3

4   5   6   7

8   9   10

Used in Games 2-1 through 2-12.

Printing half of the decks on a different-color card stock will make cleanup easier.

Number Cards 11–20

11 12 13 14

15 16 17 18

19 20

Used in Games
2-2, 2-3, and 2-12.

Printing half of
the decks on a
different-color
card stock will
make cleanup
easier.

5–9 Spinner (Games 2-6 and 2-7)

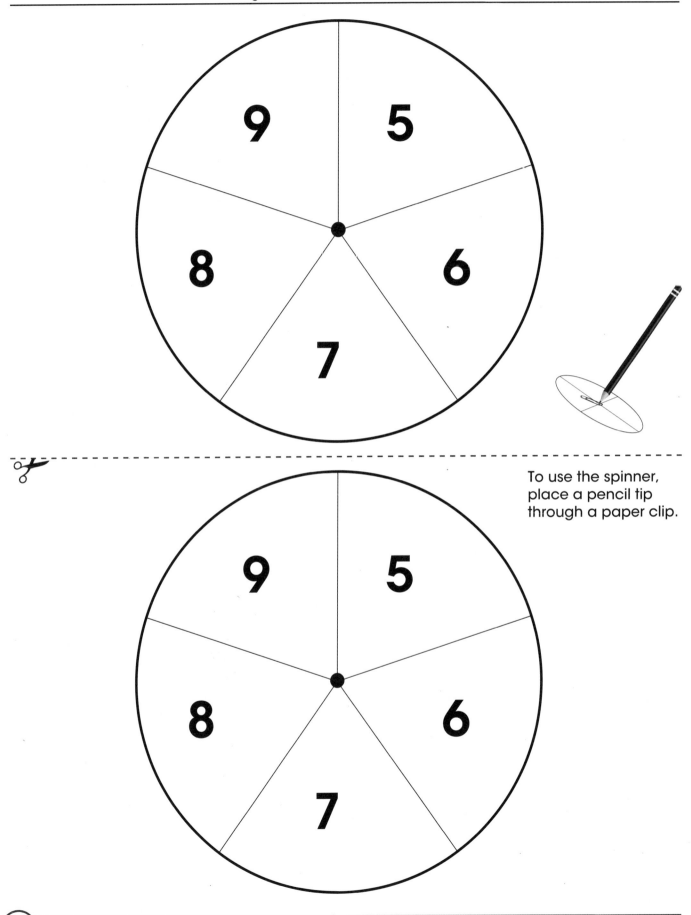

To use the spinner, place a pencil tip through a paper clip.

Hundred Chart

1	2	3	4	5	6	7	8	9	10
11	12	13	14	15	16	17	18	19	20
21	22	23	24	25	26	27	28	29	30
31	32	33	34	35	36	37	38	39	40
41	42	43	44	45	46	47	48	49	50
51	52	53	54	55	56	57	58	59	60
61	62	63	64	65	66	67	68	69	70
71	72	73	74	75	76	77	78	79	80
81	82	83	84	85	86	87	88	89	90
91	92	93	94	95	96	97	98	99	100

"Three in Any Row" Recording Sheet

(Games 2-9 and 2-10)

Player 1: _____   Player 2: _____

Round	Equations	Equations
1		
2		
3		
4		
5		
6		
7		
8		

"Fast Facts" Game

Object: Add two numbers to get the largest sum.

How to Play:

Players take turns. On your turn:

1. Draw two cards and add those numbers together.

2. Say the sum aloud. Use the Ten-Frame Cards to check your sum, If you need to.

3. If the sum is less than 11, draw another card. Keep drawing cards until your sum is 11 or more.

4. The player with the larger sum wins all the cards.

5. If it is a tie, repeat steps 1–3.

Materials

- Deck (2 sets) of Number Cards 0–10 Ten-Frame Cards

- 3 student-made "+" symbol cards for each player (optional)

Game Rules

"What's the Difference?" Game

Object: Find the difference between two numbers.

How to Play:

1. At the same time, both players draw one card from each deck.

2. Find the difference between your two numbers.

3. The player with the larger difference wins those four cards.

4. If it is a tie, draw two more cards and repeat steps 2 and 3. The winner takes all eight cards.

Materials

- Deck (2 or more sets) of Number Cards 1–10
- Deck (2 or more sets) of Number Cards 11–20
- Optional: 0–20 Number Line and paper clips to mark the numbers on the number line

Math Games for the Common Core

"What Number Do I Have?" Game

Object: Figure out the unseen number on your forehead by seeing your partner's number and knowing the sum of the two numbers.

How to Play:

1. Decide who will be the captain and who will be the two crewmembers.

2. The captain says, "Salute!"

3. If you are a crewmember, you:
   - Draw a number card.
   - Put the number card on your forehead without looking at it.

4. If you are the captain, you write down the sum of the two crewmembers' numbers and say the sum aloud.

5. If you are a crewmember, you look at the other crewmember's number, consider the sum, and figure out what number is on your own forehead.

6. The first player to correctly figure out his/her own number wins one point.

Game Rules

"Skipping Around" Game

Object: Be the first to get to the next goal by counting or by skip-counting.

Materials
- Deck (4 sets) of Number Cards 0–9
- "Skipping Around" Spinner

How to Play:

1. Decide who goes first.

2. Player 1: Turn over three cards to make a **3-digit start number.** (Zero may not be used in the hundreds place.)

3. Player 2: Spin the spinner to determine the **goal number for the round.**

    - If the spinner lands on "Ones," count by ones until there is a new number in the tens place.

    - If the spinner lands on "Tens," skip-count by tens until there is a new number in the hundreds place.

    - If the spinner lands on "Hundreds," skip-count by hundreds until there is a number over 1,000.

4. Players take turns saying the next number.

5. The first player to reach the goal number wins that round.

6. Play again. Take turns being Player 1.

Game Rules

"Everything Has Its Place" Game

Object: Create the **largest** three-digit number you can.

How to Play:

1. Players take turns. On your turn:

   • Draw 4 cards, one at a time. Place each card you draw in one column of the place value mat.

   • Once you place a card, you are not allowed to move it.

2. When you draw the 4th card, you may:

   • Choose to replace one of the cards on the place value mat with the 4th card, or

   • Discard the 4th card.

3. The player who creates the larger three-digit number wins a point.

4. Now place a symbol (<, >, =) between the numbers you and your partner have created.

5. Read the statement you made (for example, "643 is greater than 541").

6. Explain how you know the winning number is larger.

7. Play as many rounds as possible.

8. Try playing a game to create the **smallest** three-digit number.

Materials

• Deck (4 sets) of Number Cards 0–9

• Index card with ">" on one side and "=" on the other side (*Note:* Turn the "<" symbol to indicate "<" or ">.")

• Tiles or chips to represent points for winning

• Place Value Mat – Cut 8.5 by 11-inch paper in half lengthwise to make a mat. Fold each half in three sections, like a letter. Label the sections "hundreds," "tens," and "ones."

Game Rules

"Visiting Tens – Addition" Game

Object: Win the most cards by adding numbers correctly and quickly.

Materials
- Deck (2 sets) of Number Cards 1–9 for each player

How to Play:

1. Each player gets his/her own deck of cards. Use one card from each player's deck to make a two-digit **start number.**

2. Players quietly say "1, 2, 3, go" and draw another card from their decks.

3. Add that number to the start number.

4. Say the sum of the start number and the number you drew.

5. The first player to say the correct sum wins all four cards.

6. If a player says an incorrect sum, the other player wins all four cards.

7. If both players say correct sums at the same time, they turn the cards over and play another round. The winner takes all eight cards.

8. Play continues until all the cards in both decks are used. The player with the most cards wins.

9. Players may use a hundred chart or other tools to check their work after they give their answers.

"Visiting Tens – Subtraction" Game

Object: Win the most cards by subtracting numbers correctly and quickly.

How to Play:

Materials

• Deck (2 sets) of Number Cards 1–9 for each player

1. Each player gets his/her own deck of cards. Use one card from each player's deck to make a two-digit **start number.**

2. Players quietly say "1, 2, 3, go" and draw another card from their decks.

3. Subtract that number from the start number.

4. Say the difference between the start number and the number you drew.

5. The first player to say the correct difference wins all four cards.

6. If a player says an incorrect difference, the other player wins all four cards.

7. If both players say the correct differences at the same time, they turn the cards over and play another round. The winner takes all eight cards.

8. Play continues until all the cards in both decks are used. The player with the most cards wins.

9. Players may use a hundred chart or other tools to check their work after they give their answers.

"Chunks Make It Easy – Addition" Game

Object: Win the most cards by adding numbers correctly and saying the sum quickly.

Materials
- Deck (4 sets) of Number Cards 1–9
- "Chunks Make It Easy" Game Spinner

How to Play:

1. Both players: Turn over two cards and make your own smallest possible two-digit start number.

2. Player 1: Quietly say, "1, 2, 3, go," and spin the spinner.

3. Both players: Mentally add the spinner number to your own start number. Say out loud the sum of the two numbers.

4. The first player to say a correct sum wins all four start number cards.

5. If a player says an incorrect sum, the other player wins all four cards.

6. If both players say the correct sum at the same time, turn the cards over and play again. The winner takes all eight of those cards.

7. After you give your answer, you may use an open number line or hundred chart to see if you have the correct sum.

8. Play more rounds until the deck is used up.

9. The player with the most cards wins the game.

"Chunks Make It Easy" Spinner

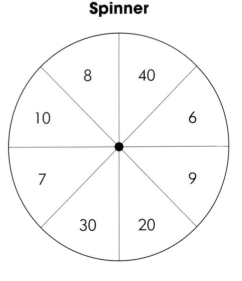

Game Rules

"Chunks Make It Easy – Subtraction" Game

Object: Win the most cards by subtracting numbers correctly and saying the difference quickly.

Materials
- Deck (4 sets) of Number Cards 1–9
- "Chunks Make It Easy" Game Spinner

How to Play:

1. Both players: Turn over two cards and make your own largest possible two-digit start number.

2. Player 1: Quietly say, "1, 2, 3, go," and spin the spinner

3. Both players: Use mental math strategies. Find the difference between the spinner number and your own start number. Say out loud the difference between the two numbers.

4. The first player to say a correct difference wins all four start number cards.

5. If a player says an incorrect difference, the other player wins all four cards.

6. If both players say the correct difference at the same time, turn the cards over and play again. The winner takes all eight of those cards.

7. After you give your answer, you may use an open number line or hundred chart to see if you have the correct difference.

8. Play more rounds until the deck is used up.

9. The player with the most cards wins the game.

"Chunks Make It Easy" Spinner

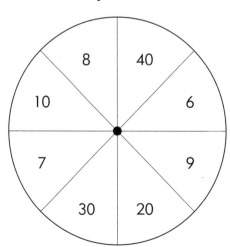

"Three in Any Row – Addition" Game

Object: Capture three numbers in any row (horizontal, vertical, or diagonal) on the game board by adding two 2-digit numbers. Numbers do not need to be next to each other.

How to Play:

1. Players take turns. On your turn:

   • Draw four cards.

   • Create two 2-digit numbers.

   • Add the two numbers together and mark the sum on the game board with your marker.

   • If you cannot make two numbers that have a sum between 1 and 100, draw another card and discard one card. Repeat, if needed.

   • Write the equation you made on the Recording Sheet.

2. Keep playing until you or your partner captures three numbers in any row, column, or on the diagonal.

Materials
• Hundred Chart (game board)
• Deck (4 sets) of Number Cards 1–9
• "Three-In-Any-Row" Recording Sheet – optional
• "Compose and Decompose" Recording Sheet – as needed for differentiation
• 2 colored markers

Advanced Version:

Same rules as above, except:

• Capture three **or more** numbers in any row (horizontal, vertical, or diagonal). Numbers must be next to each other!

"Three in Any Row – Subtraction" Game

Object: Capture three numbers in any row (horizontal, vertical, or diagonal) on the game board by subtracting two 2-digit numbers. Numbers do not need to be next to each other.

How to Play:

1. Players take turns. On your turn.

   • Draw four cards.

   • Create a 2-digit minus a 2-digit problem, or

   • Make a 2-digit minus a 1-digit problem and discard the unused card.

   • Subtract the smaller number from the larger number to get the difference.

   • Capture the difference on the game board by marking the number with your marker.

2. Keep playing until you or your partner has captured three numbers in any row, column, or on the diagonal.

Advanced Version:

Same rules as above, except:

• Capture three **or more** numbers in any row (horizontal, vertical, or diagonal). Numbers must be next to each other!

Materials
- Hundred Chart (game board)
- Deck (4 sets) of Number Cards 1–9
- Colored markers – a different color for each player
- "Three in Any Row" Recording Sheet – optional

Game Rules

"What's My Secret Number?" Game

Number of Players: 3 (1 captain and 2 crewmembers)

Object: Figure out your partner's "secret number" by subtracting or finding the missing addend.

How to Play:

1. Decide who will be the captain and who will be the crewmembers.

2. Use a privacy barrier so that the other players can't see what you are writing.

3. Crewmember 1: Write any two-digit number on two sticky notes. This is your "secret" number.

> **Materials**
>
> For each team of 3 players:
> - Deck of Number Cards 1–9
> - Tiles or chips to represent winning points
> - Hundred Chart – optional
>
> For each player:
> - Privacy barrier
> - Paper for written work
> - Sticky notes or small notepaper

4. Crewmember 2: Draw a Number Card and write that number on two sticky notes. This is your "secret" number.

5. Both crewmembers: Pass one of your notes to the captain.

6. Captain: Add the two "secret" numbers. Then say and write the sum on a piece of paper so both crewmembers can see it. (You may use a paper and pencil or a hundred chart.)

7. Crewmembers 1 and 2: Each figure out the other crewmember's secret number. To win a tile, you must be the first crewmember to:

   - Correctly say the other crewmember's secret number.

   - Show why the answer is correct.

8. Take turns being captain and crewmembers. Play again.

Game Rules

"It All Adds Up" Game

Object: Create an addition problem with three 2-digit numbers. The sum of the numbers must be as close as possible to the target number.

> **Materials**
> - Deck (4 sets) of Number Cards 1–9

How to Play: Cooperative Six-Card Version

1. You and your partner are teammates.

2. To make the target number, write "1" in the hundreds place. Then turn over a card for the tens place and another card for the ones place.

3. Draw six cards to share. Use the cards to make three 2-digit numbers with a sum as close as possible to the target number.

4. If your smallest possible sum adds up to more than 1,000, draw one more card and discard one card. Keep doing this until your smallest possible sum is less than 1,000.

5. Your score is the difference between the target number and your sum. Subtract the smaller number from the larger number.

   (Example: The target number is 245 and the sum is 257. The team scores 12 points.)

6. The team with the lowest score in the class wins the game.

How to Play: Competitive Six-Card Version

Use the Cooperative Six-Card Game Rules, except:

- You and your partner are opponents.

- You and your partner each draw six cards.

- The player with the sum closest to the target number wins.